PRAYER DIARY

BY JEANNE HINTON

FULL COLOR PLATES
BY JEAN CROSON

OLIVER-NELSON PUBLISHERS
Nashville

Published in Nashville, Tennessee, by Oliver-Nelson, Inc.,
and distributed in Canada by Lawson Falle, Ltd., Cambridge,
Ontario.

Manufactured in Singapore.

1 2 3 4 5 6 7 – 96 95 94 93 92 91

Acknowledgment of Sources

Some information and many of the prayers have been drawn from *With All God's People, an Ecumenical Prayer Cycle*.
Week 3 *With All God's People, The New Ecumenical Prayer Cycle*, p. 10. WCC Publications, Geneva 1989.
   Ibid, p. 9. Used with permission.
   21st Coptic Orthodox Patriarchate. Used with permission.
Week 9 Mother Teresa, *Contemplative in the Heart of the World*. Servant Books, USA.
   Source unknown.
Week 11 John Powell, *Why Am I Afraid to Love?* Argos Communications, USA.
Week 12 Fellowship of the Least Coin. Used with permission.
   Ibid. Used with permission.
   24th Source untraced.
Week 13 Zen saying.
Week 15 *With All God's People*, p. 238. Used with permission.
   14th Excerpted from *Prayer Calendar 1986-7*. Methodist Church Overseas Division, London.
Week 18 *Prayer for Mission*. USPG, London.
   John S Mbiti, *The Prayers of African Religion*. SPCK, London.
   5th *The World Isn't Won with Church Statistics*. St Andrews Institute, Kerugoya, Kenya.
Week 19 Julian of Norwich, *Revelations of Divine Love*. Penguin Books, England.
   Ibid.
Week 21 26th Excerpted from *1985 Prayer Calendar*. United Methodist Church, New York. Used with permission.
Week 24 16th Source untraced.
Week 27 *The Gospel According to the Ghetto*. Mambo Press, Zimbabwe.
Week 28 Ruth Burrows.
Week 29 David Augsburger, *Caring Enough to Comfort*. Herald Press, USA 1987.
Week 30 *Prayers for Peace*. SPCK, London 1987.
   28th Source untraced.
Week 32 Satish Kumar, *The Prayer for Peace*. Seniors Farm House, Shaftesbury, Dorset, England.
Week 33 *With All God's People*, p. 274. Used with permission.
   Calendar of Prayer 1986-7. United Church of Christ Board for World Ministries. Used with permission.
Week 34 *Hymns Ancient and Modern*. William Clowes & Sons Ltd, London.
   John Powell, *Happiness is an Inside Job*. Tabor Publishing, USA.
Week 36 *Hymns of Worship*. Assn. Press, New York.
   John Carden, *With All God's People*, p. 214.
   Prayers for Peace. SPCK, London 1987
   Faithful Reflections on Our Experience. Women's Inter-Church Council of Canada.
Week 39 Hallgrimur Petersson, *Hymns of the Passion*. 1674.
   With All God's People, page 67. Used with permission.
   Ibid, p. 74. Used with permission.
Week 41 *St Francis at Prayer*. DLT, London.
   Ibid.
Week 42 Aus: Barth, Karl: *Gebete. 4.Aufl.1974 (München)*. Rechte: Theologischer Verlag. Zürich.
   Swiss Protestant Church Federation, Switzerland.
Week 43 Henri J.M. Nouwen & Walter J. Gaffney, *Aging*. Image Books, New York 1976.
Week 44 Robert Faricy, S.J. & Robert J. Wicks, *Contemplating Jesus*. Paulist Press 1986.
Week 45 *The Oxford Book of Prayer*. Oxford University Press, London.
   Week of Prayer for Christian Unity 1986. British Council of Churches.
Week 49 One in Solidarity from *100 Prières Possibles*.
   Prayers, Poems and Songs. Sheed and Ward Ltd, London.
Week 51 Thomas Merton.
Week 52 *The Church is All of You*. Fount Paperbacks, London 1985.

Key to Scripture Quotations

GNB   Good News Bible
NIV   New International Version
RSV   Revised Standard Version
LB   The Living Bible

INTRODUCTION

There are three themes running through this diary. First, that of your own personal growth and prayer life; secondly, ways to nurture relationships; thirdly, that of praying for God's world.

The pages include many practical suggestions for you to consider. You are unlikely to find time to follow them all! Some of them will immediately strike you as suggestions you want to pursue. These are the ones to put into practice this year. Others will be like seeds sown for a later date. There may come the time when you will remember them, and want to return to those pages and read them again.

Every three weeks prayers are directed to different countries of the world. The information given each week is to help you use your own imagination and initiative in praying for these countries. Global situations change weekly. Seek to keep yourself up-to-date, particularly where you feel drawn to know more about a country for which you are praying. A world map or globe will be a useful aid to your praying. Prayers are included from Christians of many lands to help you pray together with them.

WEEK ONE

FIRST	GOD'S LOVING-KINDNESS BEGINS AFRESH EACH DAY / Lam 3:23 (LB)
SECOND	FORGETTING WHAT IS BEHIND, I PRESS TOWARDS THE GOAL / Phil 3.13, 14 (NIV)
THIRD	SING TO THE LORD A NEW SONG / Ps 33:3 (NIV)
FOURTH	...WHAT MATTERS IS THAT WE ARE BEING CHANGED INTO NEW AND DIFFERENT PEOPLE / Gal 6:15 (LB)
FIFTH	...BE MADE NEW IN THE ATTITUDE OF YOUR MIND / Eph 4:23 (NIV)
SIXTH	...PUT ON THE NEW SELF / Col 3:10 (NIV)
SEVENTH	SEE, I AM MAKING ALL THINGS NEW / Rev 21:5 (LB)

God is always giving us new opportunities.

When God created this world, he did so in stages. He was building into life a rhythm – night and day, weeks, months and years, different seasons – winter, spring, summer and autumn. Each of these is a reminder to stop and reflect on what is past and consider what is to come. These stopping places are God-given opportunities for setting and reviewing life goals.

The New Year is traditionally a time for making resolutions – often not kept beyond a week or two. It is a good time to set a goal or goals for the year. It is best if these are not 'should not's' – ("I should not get angry,"), but genuine 'want to's' – ("I want to learn to paint this year", or "I want to spend more time with my children"). Then you can decide how you are going to go about this, and each month review what you have actually managed to do.

This is the best way to make resolutions. New habits, new directions are rarely formed in a day or even a week. They often take a period of months.

God is very patient with us, and if we will be patient and also gently resolute, we will come nearer to achieving our life goals.

Do you have a goal or goals for this year?

In many homes this week, Christmas cards and letters will be taken down and put away. Simple tasks like this can become a way to pray. Make this an opportunity to pray for your friends and to think about the part friendship plays in your life.

Group the cards and letters into four categories: family members, friends close by, friends further away, and neighbors and acquaintances. Then, following the prayer topic for the day, take the appropriate number of cards and slowly and thoughtfully, one at a time, read the greetings or letters again and think about each person, praying for her or him and reflecting on her or his place in your life.

The topics towards the end of the week broaden this week's reflection on friendship. Regularly when praying for family members and friends, pray too for the lonely and bereaved, for newcomers to your neighborhood, for those you pass casually in the street. This can help us become more aware of the needs of others and may be the means this year of widening your circle of friends and acquaintances in some unexpected and delightful ways!

This week use these two questions to help you think about the place that friendship plays in your life.

What makes people friends?

What helps to build and sustain friendship?

PRAY FOR MEMBERS OF YOUR FAMILY — **EIGHTH**

FOR CLOSE FRIENDS — **NINTH**

FOR FRIENDS FARTHER AWAY — **TENTH**

FOR NEIGHBORS AND ACQUAINTANCES — **ELEVENTH**

FOR THE LONELY AND BEREAVED — **TWELFTH**

FOR NEWCOMERS TO YOUR NEIGHBORHOOD — **THIRTEENTH**

FOR YOURSELF AS A FRIEND TO OTHERS — **FOURTEENTH**

WEEK THREE

FIFTEENTH	PRAY FOR JERUSALEM
SIXTEENTH	FOR EGYPT
SEVENTEENTH	FOR ISRAEL AND THE OCCUPIED TERRITORIES
EIGHTEENTH	FOR JORDAN
NINETEENTH	FOR LEBANON
TWENTIETH	FOR SYRIA
TWENTY-FIRST	O GOD OF THE EVER PRESENT CROSSES, HELP US YOUR SERVANTS. (4th Century Egyptian Prayer)

Christians around the world are praying this month for Jerusalem and the countries of the Middle East.

In the "Upper Room" in Jerusalem is the figure of a pelican feeding her young with her own blood, an ancient symbol of the self-giving love of God in Christ. It is a reminder too of the way in which Jesus expressed his own love and concern for that city: "O Jerusalem! How often would I have gathered your children together as a hen gathers her brood under her wings, and you would not!" (Mt. 23:37 RSV)

Maps used by many of the medieval pilgrims to the Holy Land showed the world as centered on Jerusalem, with the continents of Africa, Asia and Europe radiating from that center. Today it is as though Jerusalem and the countries of the Middle East are at the epicenter of many of the world's conflicts – of race and religion,of the arms trade and of economic poverty and oppression.

The problems these countries face are the same ones that confront us all. A worker in a Palestinian refugee camp sums these up as threefold:

...first to comfort and relieve, then to inspire patience founded on hope, and thirdly to provide a happy issue out of affliction.

A prayer from the Middle East focuses our praying for this week:

Lord, after all the talking; questioning, agonising over your land grant that some compassionate breakthrough may occur. Amen.

Are you planning to go abroad on holiday this year?

Tourism has become one of the largest items of international trade. Europe and the Americas receive the largest percentage of tourists, but the tourist trade is now growing fast in developing countries.

Tourism is welcome as a source of foreign exchange, but can be ruinous to the local way of life and the natural environment. In many Third World countries, services and goods are cheap, but to the detriment of local people who do not receive a fair wage for their labor. In some countries tourism also encourages child prostitution and beggary. Means of travel, particularly air travel, add to environmental pollution.

However, tourism can be a means of developing international friendship and understanding, a sensitivity to each other's customs and an increased awareness of our common responsibility to care for the natural beauty of this earth which is our common home.

Travel agents know there are ethical considerations in planning travel, and there are agencies to help us plan holidays where we can learn more about local customs, and meet or stay with local people. Perhaps we should travel abroad less often, and when we do holiday abroad do so more sensitively and responsibly?

Traidcraft, a British business selling products from developing countries, suggests that "western travellers need to be a bit more humble – and see their holiday in someone else's country as a privilege rather than divine right."

THINK OF COUNTRIES YOU HAVE VISITED	**TWENTY-SECOND**
...OF THEIR NATURAL BEAUTY	**TWENTY-THIRD**
...OF LOCAL PEOPLE YOU MET	**TWENTY-FOURTH**
PRAY FOR THOSE COUNTRIES AND PEOPLE	**TWENTY-FIFTH**
WHAT COUNTRIES WOULD YOU LIKE TO VISIT?	**TWENTY-SIXTH**
WHAT MIGHT RESPONSIBLE TRAVEL MEAN FOR YOU?	**TWENTY-SEVENTH**
THANK GOD FOR SO MUCH RICHNESS AND DIVERSITY TO BE DISCOVERED IN OUR 'ONE WORLD'	**TWENTY-EIGHTH**

Candlemas is celebrated this week in many countries on 2 February – forty days after the birth of Jesus.

On this day we remember how Joseph and Mary brought the child Jesus to the temple in Jerusalem to dedicate him to God, an observance similar to that of the tradition of dedicating or baptising babies in the Christian church. At Jesus' dedication the Jewish temple would have been brightly lit by a mass of candles, which is why we remember the day as Candlemas.

Candles have always been a Christian symbol for the light that Christ brought into the world. In a poor neighborhood in Pittsburgh, Pennsylvania, in America, there is a row of houses near to a bend on a main road. Each night as darkness falls a candle shines out from each house penetrating the darkness. The members of the Christian community who live in these homes keep these candles burning throughout the night (they are lit by electricity) as a reminder that Christ came to bring light to the world.

At Candlemas, Christian families sometimes celebrate the day at home by lighting lots of candles, and then retelling the story of Jesus' dedication in the Temple. They then allow the children to stay up until one candle burns all the way down and flickers out.

A simple meditation at the end of this week would be to meditate on Jesus' call to us as Christians to be light in this world. What does this call mean to you in your life? Burn a small candle and spend a while slowly pondering this question.

GOD IS LIGHT / 1 Jn 1:5 (NIV)	**TWENTY-NINTH**
THE ENTRANCE OF YOUR WORDS GIVES LIGHT/ Ps 119:130 (NIV)	**THIRTIETH**
...A LIGHT TO MY PATH / Ps 119:105 (RSV)	**THIRTY-FIRST**
I (JESUS) AM THE LIGHT OF THE WORLD / Jn 8:12 (RSV)	**FIRST**
YOU (CHRISTIANS) ARE LIKE LIGHT / Mt 5:14 (GNB)	**SECOND**
...LIGHT BRINGS A RICH HARVEST OF EVERY KIND / Eph 5:9 (GNB)	**THIRD**
...YOU BELONG TO THE LIGHT / 1 Thess 5:5 (GNB)	**FOURTH**

WEEK SIX

FIFTH   PRAY FOR CYPRUS , GREECE, TURKEY

SIXTH   FOR ALGERIA, LIBYA

SEVENTH   FOR MOROCCO, TUNISIA

EIGHTH   FOR SAUDI ARABIA AND THE GULF STATES

NINTH   FOR IRAQ

TENTH   FOR IRAN

ELEVENTH   *KYRIE ELEISON* – LORD HAVE MERCY

Lord Jesus Christ
Son of the living God
have mercy on me
a sinner.

This simple prayer is called the "Jesus prayer", and is used by Christians throughout the world. Originating in Sinai, it has a particular association with Mount Athos in Greece, where members of the Greek Orthodox Church have preserved and used it since the 10th century. The prayer is prayed by these Christian monks with a gentle repetition, as a way of opening up the heart to God. It becomes as natural to them as breathing, a "prayer of the heart".

The word *mercy* in Greek has a richness to it which is often lost in translation. It includes every good thing that God desires for his creation. This meaning of the word *mercy* is also present in praying the shorter prayer of the Orthodox Church *Kyrie Eleison – Lord have mercy*.

Kyrie Eleison is indeed an appropriate prayer as we continue this week to pray for the lands in and bordering on the Middle East. The discovery of oil in the Gulf States of Kuwait, Bahrain, Qatar, the United Arab Emirates and Oman has brough wealth and employment to these countries of the Arabian peninsula – and conflict. With so many countries dependent on supplies of oil from this region, conflict in the Middle East touches us all.

How can we share responsibly the good gifts that God has given us in creation? This is implicit in our praying the prayer "Lord, have mercy".

Do you know your own story?

There have been times when you have shared with others where you were born, where you went to school, facts about your work and friends and interests. But how well do you know your own story? Have you ever stopped and reflected on the deeper, more hidden meaning of these facts?

A simple way to do this is to draw your "lifeline". You can make the line curved or straight or zig-zag – whichever seems most appropriate. On this line mark the major events of your life. Against each event, make a note of the year and your age.

Having drawn your lifeline, here are some questions you can ask yourself: What were the circumstances that led to these turning points or events in my life? Who were the significant people in my life at the time? How did I respond to these events? Did they help me grow as a person? What was God saying to me through these events? What patterns do I observe? And what next? What do I hope for – in the next five, ten years?

A further development of this exercise is to reflect on your life to date in its historical context. God who became incarnate in this world in the person of Jesus, works out his purposes within human history. What was happening in the world at these significant moments in my own life? Locally? Globally? How does my life connect to the broad sweep of God's purposes being worked out in history and in particular the history of our own times?

Having completed these exercises, share your insights with a friend. Telling your story to a friend will deepen your own understanding of it.

YOU SAW ME BEFORE I WAS BORN... / Ps 139:16 — **TWELFTH**

YOU KNOW EVERYTHING ABOUT ME / (v1) — **THIRTEENTH**

THANK YOU FOR MAKING ME SO WONDERFULLY COMPLEX! / (v14) — **FOURTEENTH**

...YOU ARE THINKING ABOUT ME CONSTANTLY...(v17) — **FIFTEENTH**

YOU CHART THE PATH AHEAD OF ME... (v3) — **SIXTEENTH**

SEARCH ME, AND KNOW MY HEART (v23) — **SEVENTEENTH**

LEAD ME ALONG THE PATH OF EVERLASTING LIFE (v24) (LB) — **EIGHTEENTH**

WEEK EIGHT

NINETEENTH   PRAY FOR THOSE NEXT DOOR

TWENTIETH   FOR THOSE IN YOUR STREET

TWENTY-FIRST   FOR ALL IN YOUR NEIGHBORHOOD

TWENTY-SECOND   FOR STRANGERS AND NEWCOMERS

TWENTY-THIRD   FOR THOSE WHO SERVE THE COMMUNITY

TWENTY-FOURTH   FOR THE CHURCHES

TWENTY-FIFTH   "LOVE YOUR NEIGHBOR AS YOU LOVE YOURSELF" / Lk 10:29 (NIV)

"Who is my neighbor?" the teacher asked Jesus. Jesus, in answer to this question, told the man a story. It was a story that fit exactly. What story would Jesus tell any one of us if we put that question to him?

How well do we know our neighbors, and indeed the neighborhood in which we live? Here are some simple suggestions for building neighborhood awareness, and relationships with neighbors.

Draw a map of your neighborhood, putting in as much detail as you can from memory. This is an exercise you can do together with other family members or friends. Children will enjoy joining in! How well do you know your neighborhood? What gaps are there in your knowledge?

Take a walk around the neighborhood and fill in the gaps. Have you taken a ride on a local bus recently? That often gives a new perspective. Perhaps there are public buildings or parks you have never been into. Become a local explorer. Look at billboards, collect literature, ask questions. This too can be a shared activity.

What about walking and praying for your neighborhood? This could become a regular activity and will certainly help to build neighborhood awareness.

Invite a few neighbors over for a particular occasion. The numbers invited can be quite small, but be bold and inventive! Out of your increased neighborhood awareness will come ideas that fit your particular neighborhood. A simple invitation "to meet other neighbors" is reason enough for an occasion. Many of us live in communities that are barely communities at all.

"Who is my neighbor?" Read the story again in Luke 10.

As our poor keep growing in poverty – due to the great rise in the cost of living – let us be more careful regarding the poverty of our houses. The daily needs that our poor cannot get – let us be more careful in the use of them – so that we also feel the hardship in goods, clothing, water, electricity, soap – things which our poor often go without.

These are the words of Mother Teresa of Calcutta. The work of the Sisters of Charity among the poor of India and throughout the world, move and challenge us all. Half the Indian population live at a subsistence level, and the majority of Indian Christians come from this half. They pray not only for 'daily bread', but for changes within society that will radically alter their situation.

India and the countries for which we pray this week are lands of great contrast – of extreme natural beauty, of a great strength of family life and traditions of hospitality, existing alongside religious rivalries and intense poverty. A prayer that comes from Afghanistan draws our attention to these strengths, and invites us to pray for all the peoples of this region that God's will be done "on earth as in heaven".

O Creator God,
we rejoice that the ruggedness of this land
has produced a people
of great resourcefulness and tenacity
of hospitality and diversity,
and we ask for them
a share in your new creation.

PRAY FOR AFGHANISTAN	**TWENTY-SIXTH**
FOR PAKISTAN	**TWENTY-SEVENTH**
FOR INDIA	**TWENTY-EIGHTH**
FOR SRI LANKA	**FIRST**
FOR BANGLADESH	**SECOND**
FOR BHUTAN AND NEPAL	**THIRD**
"MAY YOUR WILL BE DONE ON EARTH, AS IT IS IN HEAVEN." / Mt 6:10 (GNB)	**FOURTH**

FOURTH	I WILL BLESS THE LORD AT ALL TIMES/ Ps 34:1 (RSV)
FIFTH	THE LORD IS MY CHOSEN PORTION/ Ps 16:5 (RSV)
SIXTH	PROVE ME, O LORD, AND TRY ME/Ps 26:2 (RSV)
SEVENTH	RELIEVE THE TROUBLES OF MY HEART/Ps 26:17 (RSV)
EIGHTH	DO NOT HIDE YOUR FACE FROM ME/Ps 27:9 (LB)
NINTH	HE RESTORES MY SOUL/Ps 23:3 (RSV)
TENTH	MAY...THE MEDITATION OF MY HEART BE PLEASING IN YOUR SIGHT, O LORD/Ps 19:14 (LB)

The Psalms of David are like a spiritual journal.

Morning, noon and night I will praise you O God Ps. 119:169 (NIV).

Each day and throughout the day David sang prayers, petitions, and praise to God. In this way he recorded the major crises of his life, his ups and downs, those things for which he was grateful, and also his complaints to God.

To keep a spiritual journal or diary is a wonderful aid to prayer. It is a way to unload all the events of the day or week. It helps us gain a perspective on our journey month by month, year by year. Into our journal can go descriptions of those things which have delighted and warmed us, thoughts we have on reading the Scriptures, bits of conversations, quotations from books, our feelings about this and that. Sometimes we may feel like writing out our prayers, but all of the journal can be a conversation with God, an opening out of our lives to him.

For most of us, writing a journal is likely to be the way most natural to us. But there are many ways of journaling. David, God's troubadour, composed songs that he sang and kept. A collection of drawings, photographs, even an embroidered tapestry – all of these can be ways of recording the events of our lives. Or our journal can contain all of these: words, songs, prayers, drawings, photographs.

Each person's journal will be unique. The way you compile yours is as individual and particular as the happenings you record.

"Did you hear about...?" "Terrible weather we're having this month..."

Conversation is an essential tool of communication. From time to time it is helpful to stop and ask ourselves: how *real* is the communication?

There are many different levels of communication, and all of them are important. In a book called *Why am I Afraid to Tell You Who I Am?*, author John Powell writes about five levels: 1) 'cliche' conversation ("nice day, today"), 2) reporting the facts about others ("have you heard?"), 3) sharing ideas and judgments, 4) sharing feelings and 5) peak communication – absolute openness and honesty.

We need relationships at all these levels, and one level is a stepping stone to the other. Fear of letting myself be known at a deep level by another can stop my development of peak communication. This is a fear of being loved, and of loving.

In the Bible there is a close correlation between knowing and loving a person. If we say we are loved, we are also saying that person knows and accepts us. To love another is the same. When we begin to take risks ourselves, we also open up the way for others to love.

Think about the different levels of communication in your life. Who are those with whom you share your deepest feelings and with whom you can be absolutely open and honest? Can you dare to take a step in opening up a new level of your relationship with another person?

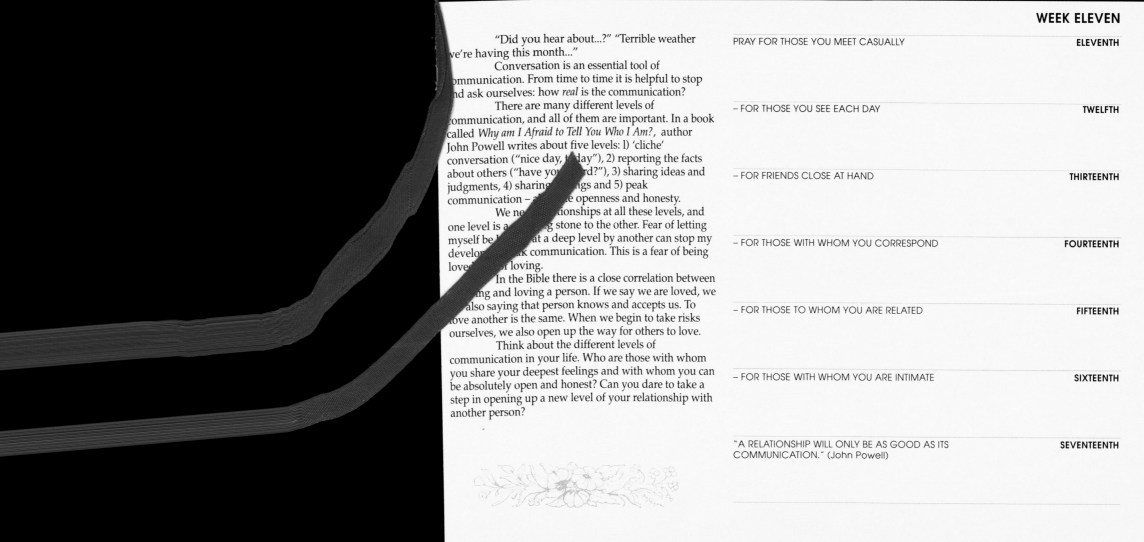

PRAY FOR THOSE YOU MEET CASUALLY — ELEVENTH

– FOR THOSE YOU SEE EACH DAY — TWELFTH

– FOR FRIENDS CLOSE AT HAND — THIRTEENTH

– FOR THOSE WITH WHOM YOU CORRESPOND — FOURTEENTH

– FOR THOSE TO WHOM YOU ARE RELATED — FIFTEENTH

– FOR THOSE WITH WHOM YOU ARE INTIMATE — SIXTEENTH

"A RELATIONSHIP WILL ONLY BE AS GOOD AS ITS COMMUNICATION." (John Powell) — SEVENTEENTH

WEEK TWELVE

EIGHTEENTH   PRAY FOR KAMPUCHEA, LAOS, VIETNAM

NINETEENTH   BURMA, THAILAND, INDONESIA

TWENTIETH   HONG KONG, MACAO, CHINA, TAIWAN

TWENTY-FIRST   JAPAN, NORTH AND SOUTH KOREA

TWENTY-SECOND   THE PHILIPPINES

TWENTY-THIRD   BRUNEI, MALAYSIA , SINGAPORE

TWENTY-FOURTH   YOUR DEATH, O LORD, WE COMMEMORATE – AMEN
YOUR GLORY AS OUR RISEN LORD, WE NOW CELEBRATE – AMEN
YOUR RETURN AS LORD IN GLORY, TOGETHER WE AWAIT – AMEN
(Prayer of Filipino Christians)

Over the last forty years, a worldwide fellowship of Christian women has been forming, the Fellowship of the Least Coin. The least of the coins symbolises that all are able to make a contribution. The idea of such a Fellowship came first from Asian women, and is of women committed to pray and work for peace and reconciliation throughout the world. As a sign of this commitment, these women regularly set aside the smallest coin of the country's currency, offering this for the needs of others along with their prayer,

> *God of peace,*
> *help us to be committed as Christians to be*
> *peacemakers.*
> *Give us the courage to speak up for truth and*
> *justice.*
> *Empower us to be Christians not only in word*
> *but in action.*
> *May your peace be achieved*
> *by the power of love, tolerance and justice.*
> *In the name of Jesus, the Prince of Peace.*
> *Amen.*

Throughout Asia the number of Christians are growing daily. Many meet not in large buildings, but in homes. This is a way of life in keeping with the early church of the New Testament, and one that enables them to support each other in the problems they face daily. A Thai Christian woman prays:

> *O God, be with us in this new day, heal the wounds made by war. Ease the suspicions that lurk in the back of the mind about people we cannot see and do not know. Prepare us for a life as full of unexpected joys as it is of unexpected sorrows.*

Jean Crosen

WEEK THIRTEEN

TWENTY-FIFTH THANK GOD FOR NEW GROWTH – IN NATURE

TWENTY-SIXTH – IN YOUR OWN LIFE

TWENTY-SEVENTH – IN OTHERS

TWENTY-EIGHTH – IN THE CHURCH

TWENTY-NINTH – IN YOUR NEIGHBORHOOD

THIRTIETH – IN SOCIETY

THIRTY-FIRST (GOD) WILL COME TO US...AS THE SPRING RAINS THAT WATER THE EARTH/Hos 6:3 (RSV)

"Spring comes and the grass grows by itself."

What are the signs you watch for that Spring has come? Do you celebrate the coming of Spring?

In the rhythm and constancy of the seasons, God is sharing with us deep truths about himself and about life. Life is never static; it is always renewing itself. The seasons speak to us of hiddenness, of newness, of fullness and of fruitfulness. Here there is both change and variety and yet constancy. To learn to celebrate nature's seasons can be a way to learn to celebrate the seasons of our own life, to grow.

Find ways this Spring to celebrate the season. One way could be to begin to compile your own "book of the seasons". This book could contain drawings, photographs, sayings, poems – your own and those of others. You can add new pages year by year, and it will add to your own enjoyment and appreciation of each season.

In our own life patterns, spring is the season of childhood and young adulthood. Spring, however, comes to us again many times throughout our lives. It comes to us in all new beginnings, fresh experiences. What is a new beginning for you this year? Are there experiences you face that are challenging or perhaps even frightening? Can you trust new growth?

Spring is a time to trust ourselves to the newness in our lives.

Your word is a light to guide me, and a light for my path. Ps 119:105 (NIV).

It is important to know God's Word as it comes to all of us in the broad sweep of the Old and New Testaments, but God's Word also comes to us in very particular and personal ways too. Which stories in the Bible do you like best, or come to mind most often? Are there particular Bible verses or passages – underlined perhaps – that have a personal meaning for you?

God's Word comes to us in other ways too. What about your favorite hymns, or songs? Perhaps just one verse or a line of a hymn or song has a special meaning for you?

God's Word comes to us with a consistency that is rooted in his intimate and loving knowledge of us. Favorite Bible stories and passages, or a verse or a line of a hymn, can tell us a lot about ourselves as well as about God.

"The person who trusts in God will not be disappointed." The person for whom this is an important verse will be encouraged by God's promise to him or her. But there is something else to look at here too. More likely than not this person is someone who has a "disappointment script". "It will always go wrong for me." "I know I will be disappointed again." God's Word is always very exact. He knows us through and through.

Take a deeper look at those favorite stories, passages and hymns again. What do you learn from them – not only about God, but about yourself?

...THE WORD OF GOD IS LIVING AND ACTIVE/Heb 4:12 (NIV)

FIRST

...A WORD IN SEASON, HOW GOOD IT IS/Prov 15:23 (RSV)

SECOND

...HE SENT FORTH HIS WORD AND HEALED THEM. Ps 197:20 (NIV)

THIRD

I HAVE...STORED (YOUR WORDS) IN MY HEART/Ps 119:11 (LB)

FOURTH

(GOD'S) WORD IS TRUTH/Jn 17:17 (NIV)

FIFTH

LET THE WORD OF CHRIST DWELL IN YOU RICHLY/Col 3:16 (NIV)

SIXTH

ALL (GOD'S) PROMISES PROVE TRUE/Ps 18:30 (LB)

SEVENTH

WEEK FIFTEEN

EIGHTH   PRAY FOR MICRONESIA

NINTH   POLYNESIA

TENTH   PAPUA NEW GUINEA

ELEVENTH   AND OTHER MELANESIAN ISLANDS

TWELFTH   NEW ZEALAND

THIRTEENTH   AUSTRALIA

FOURTEENTH   LET THE SEAS OF THE PACIFIC OCEAN CARRY MESSAGES OF PEACE
AND GOODWILL

The coconut palm is the "tree of life" for the Pacific islanders. It provides them with food and drink, clothing and shelter. It is a symbol to them of God's provision and of his working in their lives.

The Pacific is the largest ocean in the world. There are more than two thousand islands that fall into three main areas: to the north, Micronesia; to the east, Polynesia; to the west, Melanesia.

The islands were populated by many different tribes, leading to inter-tribal warfare. Today there is a growing consciousness among the islanders of their inter-dependence, and the desire to discover new ways of relating across tribal loyalties. Here too islanders have learnt lessons from the coconut palm – the indigenous "coconut palm theology" uses the way that the seeds are carried from island to island to teach that God's way is that of inter-dependence.

Co-operation with others has not always been to the islanders' advantage. Some islands have been used by foreign powers for the testing of nuclear weapons and the dumping of nuclear waste. This is a threat to their main means of survival, fishing, and many islanders suffer from the effects of radiation. Here, too, the coconut palm is a symbol – of Jesus' identification with them in their suffering. This is symbolized by marking the coconut with a cross, and then it is kicked, rolled and finally hacked with a knife. The water and meat of the coconut is then used to celebrate the Lord's Supper.

The prayer of a Tahitian pastor sums this up:

"O Lord, our palm trees can no longer hide us from the world. Strengthen our hearts that we may look with confidence at the future."

"I'm sorry. What did you just say?"

How many times do we really listen to another? More often than not when another person is speaking, our thoughts are on what we are going to say in reply, or wandering off to think about this or that other thing. Or we are waiting for that person to stop talking, in order to put our bit into the conversation. As a result, few of us ever feel we are really heard by another. A lot of loneliness has to do with a person not feeling really heard.

Think about the conversations you have had in the past week. Did that person have your full attention? Could you have repeated back to them what they said to you? Sometimes it is a good exercise to do just that in order to check out that we heard and understood what was being said to us.

If your full attention is on the other person, you will begin to hear not only what they are saying in words, but what they are not saying. You will notice that the way they look and stand is conveying as much as the words they are speaking. In seeking to hear what that person is really wanting to share, you will know what questions to ask to continue to draw them out. You will know too when to stop, when to be silent.

The gift of listening to another is one of the greatest gifts we can offer another.

LISTEN TO THE SOUNDS AROUND YOU — FIFTEENTH

– TO WORDS THAT ARE SAID — SIXTEENTH

– TO WORDS THAT ARE NOT SAID — SEVENTEENTH

– TO CHILDREN — EIGHTEENTH

– TO THOSE WHO HAVE DIFFICULTY COMMUNICATING — NINETEENTH

– BY TREATING CONFIDENCES WITH RESPECT — TWENTIETH

PRAY FOR THOSE YOU HAVE LISTENED TO THIS WEEK. — TWENTY-FIRST

WEEK SEVENTEEN

TWENTY-SECOND   TODAY BE AWARE OF ALL YOU CAN SEE

TWENTY-THIRD   ... OF ALL YOU CAN HEAR

TWENTY-FOURTH   ... OF ALL YOU CAN TOUCH

TWENTY-FIFTH   ... OF ALL YOU CAN SMELL

TWENTY-SIXTH   ... OF ALL YOU CAN TASTE

TWENTY-SEVENTH   TAKE A SENSE WALK

TWENTY-EIGHTH   CAPTURE YOUR EXPERIENCE IN WRITING OR BY DRAWING

It is a beautiful spring day. Do you sometimes take an unplanned walk for no other reason than to enjoy God's creation?

Perhaps you have a favorite walk near home, or in the countryside nearby. What about taking a "sense walk"? This is a walk when you consciously exercise all five senses: seeing, hearing, touching, smelling and even tasting.

Take this walk very slowly and reflectively. Start by using your sense of sight. Name all that you see around you. Look for the unexpected – what you would normally have missed if you had not taken the time to stop and look. Then move on to all the sounds you can hear. Name them. Now move on to touching. Feel the fresh air on your skin. Breathe deeply and feel its coolness as you breathe in, the warm air as you breathe out. Feel the ground under your feet, and sense how your body feels as it moves. What can you smell? What scents are there? Now feel the texture of the grass, the plants, the bark of a tree. Feel, smell – and if appropriate, taste. Is the taste sweet or bitter? Having exercised all five senses., continue your walk slowly, allowing each sense to respond to what is around you.

At home you could write about your experience in prose or poetry. Or draw or paint a picture; perhaps of a bunch of flowers and grasses you have collected on the way. Return a second time to this same place and take a camera with you, and see how much of your walk you can capture with photographs. In this way you can respond to each season as it comes, and add these pieces to your "book of the seasons".

May Africa praise you, you the true God
from the south even to the north,
from east to west, from sea to sea.
May the mighty wind bear your name
through cities and hamlets,
by quiet valleys and silent mountains,
over moving waters and sounding falls,
across the sunlit desert,
over the quivering savannah,
through the mysterious forest.
Across the immense African land, overflowing
*   with your praise,*
imprint all with your splendour which words
*   cannot express.*
May your name be known and loved over all
*   the land.*
        (Jerome Bala)

This prayer for Africa captures for us its rich beauty, and the closeness of the African peoples to the land. The land is, however, dependent on rain for its harvests, and increasing drought brings famine and disruption to the people of Africa. As we pray with the African people for the rain they need, we need to remember that global warming is one possible cause of worsening climactic conditions in Africa. As peoples of the world we are connected in ways never considered before.

O God, give us rain,
we are in misery, we suffer with our children.
Send us the clouds that bring the rain.
We pray thee, O Lord, our Father,
to send us the rain.
        (Church of the Province of Kenya)

PRAY FOR DJIBOUTI, ETHIOPIA — **TWENTY-NINTH**

SOMALIA — **THIRTIETH**

THE SUDAN, UGANDA — **FIRST**

KENYA, TANZANIA — **SECOND**

MADAGASCAR, MALAWI — **THIRD**

ZAMBIA — **FOURTH**

MAY THE FIELDS BEAR MUCH FRUIT AND THE LAND BE FERTILE — **FIFTH**

He showed me a little thing, the size of a hazelnut, in the palm of my hand, and it was as round as a ball. I looked at it with my mind's eye and I thought, "What can this be?" An answer came *"It is all that is made."* I marvelled that it could last, for I thought it might have crumbled to nothing, it was so small. And the answer came into my mind, *"It lasts and ever shall because God loves it..."* In this little thing I saw three truths. The first is that God made it. The second is that God loves it. The third is that God looks after it.

Julian of Norwich, who wrote these words, was an English mystic, revered by many as a saint. She lived through calamitous days in the late Middle Ages, and yet her own experience of God led her to a deep trust in God's ability to look after what he has made and loves. As a young woman she had a number of visions or "shewings" of Jesus, on which she meditated for the next twenty years before writing them down. Her *Revelations of Divine Love* is thought to be the first book written in English by a woman.

Today there is an increased interest in Julian around the world, for her experience of God speaks directly to needs of our own times. Her best known saying is: *"The cause of all this pain is sin. But all shall be well, and all shall be well, and all manner of things shall be well."*

Julian is remembered this month on May 8 and the day-to-day sayings are taken from her writings.

IN HIS LOVE, HE ENFOLDS...AND EMBRACES US — **SIXTH**

HE LOVES AND ENJOYS US — **SEVENTH**

HE WANTS US TO SEE AND ENJOY EVERYTHING IN LOVE — **EIGHTH**

PRAYER FASTENS THE SOUL TO GOD — **NINTH**

IF WE FALL WE ARE TO GET UP QUICKLY — **TENTH**

NOTHING SHALL FAIL OF HIS PURPOSE — **ELEVENTH**

ALL OUR LORD DOES IS RIGHT, AND WHAT HE PERMITS IS WORTHWHILE — **TWELFTH**

WEEK TWENTY

THIRTEENTH   THANK GOD FOR VARIETY – IN CREATION

FOURTEENTH   – OF CULTURES

FIFTEENTH   – OF PEOPLES

SIXTEENTH   – OF TEMPERAMENT

SEVENTEENTH   – OF SKILLS

EIGHTEENTH   – OF VOCATIONS

NINETEENTH   THE SPIRIT'S PRESENCE IS SHOWN IN SOME WAY IN EACH PERSON
FOR THE GOOD OF ALL/1 Cor 12:7 (GNB)

What kind of person are you?

Are you outgoing, someone who likes parties and having lots of people around, or someone who prefers a quiet evening on your own or with just one or two close friends? Are you someone who uses your eyes and ears a lot, or a person who is more often lost in thought? Do you look more at the facts of a situation or at how people feel about it? Do you like to have prearranged plans, or do you avoid fixed plans?

Our personality has a lot to say about how we relate to others, what kind of jobs most suit us, and also what kind of prayer will most help us grow in relationship to God: expressive, quiet, or focused prayer. To help each other discover the differences in personality is to free each other to grow.

What are the differences between us? With close friends or with members of your family, talk about the different ways you relate to people, tasks, decisions, plans, prayer.

Often others have expected us to be the same as them. And we expect it of others too. We need to learn to celebrate differences.

Ezigbo hwannem, nyem aka gi
Ezigbo hwannem, myem obi gi

Immediately this blessing is said at the end of a service in a Nigerian church, one member will begin to sing this refrain.

My good brother/sister, give me your hand,
My good brother/sister, give me your heart.

The refrain is taken up by others in the congregation, and as they move out of the church they move around shaking hands with one another. They continue singing as they move outside the church; their chorus of farewell a witness of the bonds of Christian love.

African Christians extend this same warmth of greeting to all fellow Christians they meet of whatever nationality. Human relationships are given a high priority over other things; time spent greeting each other and sharing news is never time wasted.

In continuing to pray for Africa this week, pray for political stability, improvements to the economy, developments in the fields of education and health, and for those who visit these countries as tourists that they may meet and build strong relationships with the people of these countries.

PRAY FOR LIBERIA, SIERRA LEONE	**TWENTIETH**
CAPE VERDE, GUINEA, GUINEA BISSAU	**TWENTY-FIRST**
SENEGAL, THE GAMBIA	**TWENTY-SECOND**
BENIN, GHANA	**TWENTY-THIRD**
IVORY COAST, TOGO	**TWENTY-FOURTH**
NIGERIA	**TWENTY-FIFTH**
MAY GOD GIVE YOU A LONG LIFE, A WELL BODY, AND A COOL HEART (Peace. African Blessing)	**TWENTY-SIXTH**

WEEK TWENTY-TWO

TWENTY-SEVENTH	(GOD) RESTED FROM ALL HIS WORKS/Gen 2:2 (NIV)
TWENTY-EIGHTH	BE STILL, AND KNOW THAT I AM GOD/Ps 46:10 (NIV)
TWENTY-NINTH	I HAVE STILLED AND QUIETED MY SOUL/Ps 131:2 (NIV)
THIRTIETH	(JESUS) WENT INTO THE HILLS TO PRAY/Mk 6:46 (NIV)
THIRTY-FIRST	COME...YOU WILL FIND REST FOR YOUR SOULS/Mt 11:29 (NIV)
FIRST	HE LEADS ME BESIDE QUIET WATERS/Ps 23:3 (NIV)
SECOND	BETTER IS A HANDFUL OF QUIETNESS THAN TWO HANDS FULL OF TOIL/Eccl 4:6 (RSV)

How many "stopping places" do you have in your life?

If you are on a long hike or climbing a hill or mountain, you would pace yourself. Occasionally you would stop and rest before going any farther. Time to look back at the way you've come, to consult the map as to the next part of the journey. Time too to stretch out and rest, to have a snack, perhaps even to camp for the night.

Our life is like a journey or an ascent. To pace ourselves is sensible; to build in such "stopping places". An hour or so once a week, an afternoon or evening once a month, a weekend or week once or twice a year.

A holiday may or may not be such a stopping place. Such a place is time just for you – away from friends, family, work, chores, dogs and cats! You may need to ask other family members or friends to cover home responsibilities for you, but with imagination and ingenuity such times can usually be arranged.

This is time to look over the past week or month or year: the outer happenings, and even more significantly what's been happening and growing inside – your "inner self". Time to review goals, to look ahead. And to do so in a relaxed way – time to enjoy yourself, rest, breathe deep.

If you are keeping a spiritual journal or diary, it will come in useful at these times. To have a "soul friend" too with whom you can share your journey, who can reflect back what you are sharing, help you to clarify goals, bring a different perspective, pray with and for you, is invaluable. Seek out such "a friend", one whose wisdom and spiritual maturity you respect.

"I don't seem to be able to pray any more."
"Somewhere I've got stuck in my relationship with God."

All of us experience times like this. It happens with all relationships – times when relating is difficult, when there is a barrier to the easy flow of communication. Maybe there is something to say we're sorry for, or maybe it is time to try something new.

What about writing God a letter? You might want to write a letter about a specific matter that is important to you now or that is bothering you. Or write, as to a friend, telling him about your life as it is at present. You could then write an answer back – from God to you! After all prayer is meant to be a dialogue between us and God.

This idea of a dialogue can be followed through in another way too. Sit down in a comfortable chair, and have another empty chair there beside you. Imagine Jesus is sitting in that other chair. What would you like to talk to Jesus about? Have a conversation with him. Again you might find it helpful to write down your conversation in dialogue.

There are so many ways of learning to communicate with God. From time to time try something new. You will learn which ways work best for you, and you can build these into your own special personal way of relating.

BEFORE THEY CALL I WILL ANSWER/Is 65:24 (NIV)   **THIRD**

LORD, LET MY CRY FOR HELP COME TO YOU/Ps 102:1 (NIV)   **FOURTH**

ASK, AND YOU WILL RECEIVE/Jn 16:24 (NIV)   **FIFTH**

IF ANY OF YOU LACKS WISDOM, HE SHOULD ASK GOD/Jam 1:5 (NIV)   **SIXTH**

HE DELIVERED THEM FROM THEIR DISTRESS/Ps 107:6 (NIV)   **SEVENTH**

YOU, O LORD, HAVE HELPED ME AND COMFORTED ME/Ps 86:17 (NIV)   **EIGHTH**

YOUR FATHER IN HEAVEN (GIVES) GOOD THINGS TO THOSE WHO ASK HIM/Mt 7:11 (GNB)   **NINTH**

WEEK TWENTY-FOUR

TENTH — PRAY FOR BURKINA FASO, CHAD

ELEVENTH — MALI, MAURITANIA, NIGER

TWELFTH — CAMEROON, CENTRAL AFRICAN REPUBLIC

THIRTEENTH — CONGO, EQUATORIAL GUINEA

FOURTEENTH — GABON, SAO TOME AND PRINCIPE

FIFTEENTH — BURUNDI, RWANDA, ZAIRE

SIXTEENTH — O GOD, ENLARGE MY HEART
(Prayer of an African Christian)

O Saviour of the world,
who by your cross and precious blood
has redeemed us;
Save us and help us,
we humbly beseech you, O Lord.

The East African Revival began in Rwanda in 1929, spreading rapidly to all parts of East Africa and beyond Africa to other parts of the world. The message of walking in the light with one another as Christians, and of experiencing that the blood of Jesus cleanses us from all sin was a central theme of this revival. The influence of the revival is still felt in the countries we pray for this week, but increasingly Christians feel the challenge to integrate evangelism with social concern and action – to demonstrate what this kind of repentance means in the practicalitiies of life today.

Pray for faith and fortitude for these peoples, for all refugees from war and drought, for the rural poor, for new co-operative ventures, for a responsible and creative use of outside aid, and for Christian witness to God's love and concern for all in their everyday lives.

May the brokenness of our Lord Jesus Christ
and the Calvary love of God
and the fellowship of the Holy Spirit
be with us all. Amen.
(Revival grace)

"All Americans are loud."

"All Italians are emotional."

"All English people are snooty."

Have you ever caught yourself making a statement like that? Next time, stop and ask yourself why you feel that way. Is it a feeling you picked up from parents or at school or from the media? Stay with your feelings; don't deny them. If you made that kind of statement, even as a joke, then for you there is truth in it. Face up to the fact that you are prejudiced.

Prejudice builds walls between people, groups and nations. It leads to distrust, conflict and even war. We are all colored by the family into which we are born, the nation of which we are a part. This plays a part in my becoming the person I am, the way I reflect God's image. But all of us are made in God's image. Prejudice blinds us to this.

Jesus told a story about prejudice. In telling the story of the good Samaritan, he exposed prejudice. To those who listened, no Samaritan was good. Their prejudice had kept them from fulfilling God's command to be a good neighbor.

Jesus then took his disciples into Samaria to meet those they despised. Real personal encounter breaks down the walls of prejudice.

What walls are keeping you from being a neighbor to others? What steps can you take to break them down?

PRAY FOR THOSE WHO ARE DIFFERENT — **SEVENTEENTH**

– FOR THOSE YOU DON'T UNDERSTAND — **EIGHTEENTH**

– FOR THOSE YOU DISMISS — **NINETEENTH**

– FOR THOSE YOU AVOID — **TWENTIETH**

– FOR THOSE WHO MAKE YOU FEEL AWKWARD — **TWENTY-FIRST**

– FOR THOSE YOU FEAR — **TWENTY-SECOND**

LOVE DRIVES OUT FEAR/1 John 4:18 (NIV) — **TWENTY-THIRD**

WEEK TWENTY-SIX

TWENTY-FOURTH YOU MADE ME BOLD AND STOUT-HEARTED/Ps 138:3 (NIV)

TWENTY-FIFTH ...IN ALL THINGS GROW UP/Eph 4:15 (NIV)

TWENTY-SIXTH MAY GOD...STRENGTHEN YOU...IN YOUR INNER BEING/Eph 3:16 (NIV)

TWENTY-SEVENTH EACH ONE SHOULD CARRY HIS OWN LOAD/Gal 6:5 (NIV)

TWENTY-EIGHTH ...USING THE MIGHTY STRENGTH WHICH CHRIST SUPPLIES/Col 1:29 (GNB)

TWENTY-NINTH MAY THE LORD MAKE YOUR LOVE TO GROW AND OVERFLOW/1 Thess 3:12 (LB)

THIRTIETH ...STRAINING TOWARDS WHAT IS AHEAD/Phil 3:13 (NIV)

A day comes when it is no longer spring. Summer has come. It is different each year, but when it comes we recognise it. Perhaps it is the first day we wear a T-shirt instead of a sweater, or lie out in the sun and bask in its warmth.

Summer beckons us with its delights, an abundance of light, colour and scent. It is a season to celebrate the senses, the outdoors, to enjoy using our bodies, to relax, to play. This too is a part of the rhythm of life.

But summer has another face. It calls us to work as well as to play. The grass that in the spring grew by itself, now needs to be cut. If we do not cut back some of the growth, if we do not water our gardens, if we do not take care to protect ourselves from the sun's rays, we will learn that there are some tasks God will not do for us. It is in work and play that we discover for ourselves the meaning that summer has for us; our life's vocation both to be and to do.

Summer in our own life patterns is the season of becoming an adult. For all of us this is a lifelong task. At any age we may be mature in some things, but childish in others. Are you able to share yourself deeply with others; to make commitments you can keep? Have you discovered what you alone can initiate, bring into being, and are you taking responsibility for that yourself? What are your values, and what is important for you in life, what gives it meaning?

Summer is a time to ask ourselves how committed we are to becoming a full human being.

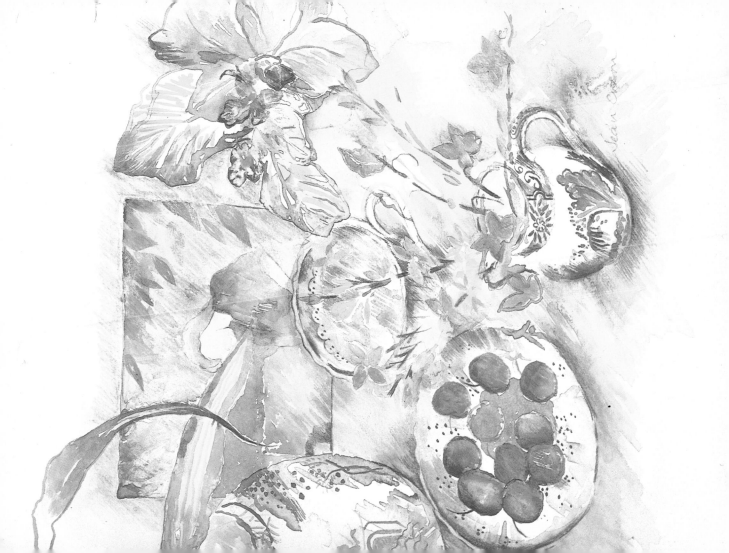

WEEK TWENTY-SEVEN

FIRST	PRAY FOR ANGOLA, MOZAMBIQUE
SECOND	BOTSWANA
THIRD	ZIMBABWE
FOURTH	SWAZILAND, LESOTHO
FIFTH	NAMIBIA
SIXTH	SOUTH AFRICA
SEVENTH	THANK YOU GOD, THAT YOU CARE

The time has come. The moment of truth has arrived... It is the kairos or moment of truth not only for apartheid, but also for the church.
Kairos Document, 1985

Throughout Southern Africa the percentage of Christians to those of other religious faiths in high, between 70 and 90 per cent of the population. Not only in South Africa, but throughout the whole region this is a moment of truth for the Christian church, and for the most part the church has risen to this kairos moment and witnessed in practical ways to God's concern for justice and reconciliation for all the people. This is no easy task, but the struggle has led to a deeper faith in the God who is always alongside.

A prayer of the Rev. Canaan Banana, First President of Zimbabwe, sums this up:

*Open my eyes that they may see the deepest needs
    of people;
Move my hands that they may feed the hungry;
Touch my heart that it may bring warmth to the
    despairing;
Teach me the generosity that welcomes strangers;
Let me share my possessions to clothe the naked
Give me the care that strengthens the sick,
Make me share in the quest to set the prisoner free;
In sharing our anxieties and our love,
our poverty and our prosperity,
we partake of your divine presence.*

"Holiness has to do with very ordinary things."

Perhaps we think that the important thing with God is spending a large amount of time praying or reading the Bible, more time that we seem able to find within our busy lives. We may constantly think of how we can organise our lives better in order to find more time for this. But these times quietly spent with God make us more mindful of God's love for us and of the way his goodness is shown to us in the very ordinary things of life.

Over two-thirds of our time is normally spent in doing very ordinary things – sleeping, washing, preparing and eating meals, doing various chores, sitting on a train or driving a car, studying, working. If we are aware of it, God can be found in all of these activities. Is it not important to be awake to his presence in this way when so much of our time is taken up in just these ordinary things? To become aware of this is to wake up indeed to the kind of celebration of living that God intended for us.

The secret of learning this kind of mindfulness is not to hurry too much over any task or to begrudge how we spend our time. There is a way, for example, to wash the dishes that makes the task enjoyable. This week take time over such ordinary chores of daily life. Don't rush through the day; enjoy all that is in it. God shares his life with you in all of his creation, and through his gift of time.

EVERYTHING WE HAVE HAS COME FROM YOU/1 Chron 29:14 (LB)   **EIGHTH**

GIVE US EACH DAY OUR DAILY BREAD/Luke 11:3 (NIV)   **NINTH**

IN ALL YOUR WAYS ACKNOWLEDGE HIM/Prov 3:6 (NIV)   **TENTH**

DO ALL...IN THE NAME OF THE LORD JESUS/Col 3:17 (NIV)   **ELEVENTH**

GIVE THANKS IN ALL CIRCUMSTANCES/1 Thess 5:18 (NIV)   **TWELFTH**

WHATEVER IS GOOD...COMES TO US FROM GOD/Jam 1:17 (LB)   **THIRTEENTH**

(CHRIST) FILLS EVERYTHING IN EVERY WAY/Eph 1:23 (NIV)   **FOURTEENTH**

WEEK TWENTY-NINE

FIFTEENTH	TRUST IN THE BASIC STUFF OF ALL RELATIONSHIPS
SIXTEENTH	FREEDOM COMES AS ONE IS CANDID AND OPEN...
SEVENTEENTH	RISK SHARING BOTH SIDES OF YOURSELF
EIGHTEENTH	TRUTH WITH LOVE BRINGS HEALING
NINETEENTH	REPENTANCE IS OWNING RESPONSIBILITY
TWENTIETH	PEACEMAKING PROCEEDS BY INVITING THE PAST TO PASS
TWENTY-FIRST	LOVE IS SEEING ANOTHER AS PRECIOUS, JUST AS YOU KNOW YOURSELF TO BE PRECIOUS

Do you care enough about others to care-front? To care-front is to learn a creative way through conflict.

You may be someone who is careful never to get into an argument with another, or conversely a person who always wins an argument. Care-fronting is to learn how to express our own thoughts and opinions and also let the other person know we care about them, to say not only what we think but how we feel.

Underlying how we think about a matter is how we feel about it. When we let another person know how we feel, we open up the conversation and our relationship to a deeper level of relating. A parent may shout, "You stayed out too late last night." He or she could say instead "I felt anxious about you last night." Then it is possible to talk about the anxiety, which is the real issue.

In his book *Caring Enough to Confront* David Augsberger identifies five ways in which we usually respond to situations of conflict: 1) I win, you lose stance; 2) I want out, I withdraw attitude; 3) I'll give in for good relations; 4) I'll meet you halfway; 5) I can care and confront.

Which of these five ways of responding to conflict is nearest to your style? In what situations do you encounter conflict, and with whom? Are there ways in which you can move towards *care*-fronting: expressing your concerns and ideals, and at the same time letting the other person know you care as much about them.

The day-to-day sayings this week are from *Caring Enough to Confront*.

On the frontier between Argentina and Chile is a monument, a pledge of peace between these two countries. This is the statue Christ of the Andes. Max Warren, a former General Secretary of the Church Missionary Society, wrote about this statue:

> *The Christ of the Andes is no longer a statue, but is taking flesh and blood in the tormented struggles of the peoples of Latin America.*

In all these countries Christians are gathering together in small communities to read the Bible and look for ways in which they can put into practice Jesus' message of "good news for the poor". They are discovering that together they can take action to improve living conditions in the areas where they live, but in taking such action they often are seen as a threat by oppressive authorities. For many in these communities this has meant persecution, imprisonment and even death.

This week pray for Christians who take action in this way, for a restoration of civil liberties where lacking, for a just solution to the crippling problem of international debt, and that natural resources may be effectively used to the benefit of all.

With Christians throughout the world we pray for the nations and peoples of Latin America, who thirst for justice and peace, longing for fuller self-determination, striving against oppression and unjust economic and social conditions and the worst kinds of poverty, yet discovering your ways of salvation in a preferential love for the poor and in the search for a just peace. World Day of Prayer for Peace, Assisi

PRAY FOR BRAZIL	**TWENTY-SECOND**
ARGENTINA	**TWENTY-THIRD**
CHILE	**TWENTY-FOURTH**
BOLIVIA	**TWENTY-FIFTH**
PARAGUAY, URUGUAY	**TWENTY-SIXTH**
PERU	**TWENTY-SEVENTH**
O GOD, TO THOSE WHO HAVE HUNGER GIVE BREAD, AND TO US WHO HAVE BREAD GIVE THE HUNGER FOR JUSTICE. (Prayer from Latin America)	**TWENTY-EIGHTH**

WEEK THIRTY-ONE

TWENTY-NINTH ...A LONGING FULFILLED IS A TREE OF LIFE/Prov 13:12 (NIV)

THIRTIETH ...TO EACH ONE OF US, GRACE HAS BEEN GIVEN/Eph 4:7 (NIV)

THIRTY-FIRST GOD HAS GIVEN EACH OF YOU SOME SPECIAL ABILITIES/1 Pet 4:10 (LB)

FIRST GOD IS AT WORK IN YOU/Phil 2:13 (RSV)

SECOND (THE LORD) ...GENEROUSLY GIVES HIS RICHES TO ALL THOSE WHO ASK/Rom 10:12 (LB)

THIRD ....HE WILL GIVE YOU THE DESIRES OF YOUR HEART/Ps 37:4 (LB)

FOURTH YOU OPEN YOUR HAND AND SATISFY THE DESIRE OF EVERY LIVING THING/Ps 145:16 (NIV)

"I wish I could be like that."
"You are so talented."
"I wish I could do that too."

Have you ever had such thoughts? They may be a clue to your own potential. All of us have more potential than we will ever realise. We will never exhaust the abundance of the gifts that God has given to each of us, but we may well through false modesty or fear hardly begin to draw on them. All of us need to learn how to "rekindle the gift of God" (2 Tim.1:6 RSV) that is within us.

Who are the people you admire most? Who has influenced you? In your reading of the Bible and other literature, who are the characters you are most drawn to? Make a list of those characteristics or skills that you admire in these people. Often we are attracted to others because they mirror a part of ourselves that we have not yet "owned".

What are your dreams? What are some wishes you had as a child or teenager that are still unfulfilled? "I wish I could..." Finish that sentence for yourself. What are the skills and talents you envy most in others? "I wish I could do that too..." Make a list of these wishes too.

Now look at what you have written. From these lists what strikes you as being particularly apt for now? Start there. God's timing in our lives is always exactly right, but he will not do for us what we need to do for ourselves.

Throughout the world August 6 is kept as Hiroshima Day.

That day on which the first atom bomb was dropped, killing more than 100,000 men, women, and children in one city, stands as a stark reminder that weapons of modern warfare have changed forever the nature of war. Albert Einstein, who helped to develop the bomb and later regretted it, commented, "The unleashed power of the atom has changed everything but our thinking".

We can all pray for a change in our way of thinking:

Lead me from Death to Life
from Falsehood to Truth
Lead me from Despair to Hope
from Fear to Trust
Lead me from Hate to Love
from War to Peace
Let Peace fill our Heart
our World, our Universe
Peace Peace Peace

In praying this prayer we start first with ourselves and then move out to pray for others and for peace in the world. This prayer for peace is used by many worldwide, and many also stop every day at midday to pray in this way.

This week reflect on this prayer and on the Scriptures, day by day. In what ways is God calling you to become a peacemaker? Committing yourself to pray regularly this prayer for peace could be a part of that.

BLESSED ARE THE PEACEMAKERS/Mt 5:9 (NIV) — **FIFTH**

MAKE EVERY EFFORT TO LIVE IN PEACE/1 Thess 5:5 (NIV) — **SIXTH**

THE FRUIT OF RIGHTEOUSNESS WILL BE PEACE/Is 32:17 (NIV) — **SEVENTH**

SEEK PEACE, AND PURSUE IT/Ps 34:14 (NIV) — **EIGHTH**

THE FRUIT OF THE SPIRIT IS PEACE/Gal 5:22 (NIV) — **NINTH**

...AND ON EARTH, PEACE/Lk 2:14 (NIV) — **TENTH**

(PRAY) THAT WE MAY LEAD PEACEFUL AND QUIET LIVES/1 Tim 2:2 (NIV) — **ELEVENTH**

O Lord, I don't want to be a spectator
A tour passenger looking out upon the real world,
An audience to poverty and want and
    homelessness,
Lord, involve me – call me –
    implicate me – commit me –
And Lord – help me to step off the bus.

This prayer is the response of one tourist, Freda Rajotte, to visiting Venezuela.

On the wall of a church in Mexico another prayer is written:

Give us, Senor, a little sun, a little happiness
    and some work.
Give us a heart to comfort those in pain.
Give us the ability to be good, strong, wise and free
    so that we may be generous with others as we
    are with ourselves.
Finally, Senor, let us all live in your own, one
    family.

People throughout the world pray very similar prayers. Jesus himself taught us to pray for our daily bread, for the strength to do good and to resist evil, and to ask forgiveness where we fail.

In continuing to focus our prayers this week on Latin America, we pray particularly for the victims of poverty and political violence – the many children who live on the streets, for young people and others caught up in the sale and use of drugs, for young women who take to prostitution, for families who wait in hope for news of disappeared family members.

PRAY FOR COLUMBIA, PANAMA — **TWELFTH**

VENEZUELA, ECUADOR — **THIRTEENTH**

BELIZE, GUATEMALA — **FOURTEENTH**

HONDURAS, COSTA RICA — **FIFTEENTH**

NICARAGUA, EL SALVADOR — **SIXTEENTH**

MEXICO — **SEVENTEENTH**

LORD, INVOLVE ME — **EIGHTEENTH**

WEEK THIRTY-FOUR

NINETEENTH	HAPPINESS IS A NATURAL CONDITION
TWENTIETH	WE MUST ACCEPT OURSELVES AS WE ARE
TWENTY-FIRST	WE MUST MAKE OUR LIVES AN ACT OF LOVE
TWENTY-SECOND	WE MUST SEEK GROWTH, NOT PERFECTION
TWENTY-THIRD	WE MUST LEARN TO COMMUNICATE EFFECTIVELY
TWENTY-FOURTH	WE MUST MAKE PRAYER A PART OF OUR DAILY LIVES
TWENTY-FIFTH	WE MUST STRETCH BY STEPPING OUT OF OUR COMFORT ZONES

Drop thy still dews of quietness,
Till all our strivings cease;
Take from our souls the strain and stress,
And let our ordered lives confess
The beauty of thy peace.

These are words from a well-known hymn. Modern life does not help us much here. To counter this, we have to take responsibility for our own lives.

Stress enters our lives through our environment, through our bodies and through our mind and spirit.

We cannot control all that is outside us in our environment, but we can create beauty around us – in our home, our room, our desk, even our car. Each of us will do that differently. See that you have around you those things that help you relax, laugh...feel at home.

We can be responsible for our own bodies, for knowing what our own needs are, for sleep, relaxation, exercise and healthy eating.

We can take responsibilty for what goes on in our own mind and within our spirit. Again, each of us is different. Some of us struggle with anxiety, others with envy; some with anger, others with greed. All of these cause stress; they rob us of beauty. Like all robbers, they do their work best in the dark. Hide them away, disown them even, and their power increases. Bring them into the open – in the pages of your journal in conversation with God, or in conversation with a trusted friend, and their power diminishes.

Bestselling author John Powell believes "Happiness is an inside job". Each of us must pursue it for ourselves. The day-to-day sayings this week are seven practises he advocates.

To Paul both to be unmarried and to be married were gifts from God: "Each one has a special gift from God". 1 Cor 7:7 (GNB)

Jesus in his own life showed that a single person can know as much and more about the depths of loving and self-giving as any married person. This was true, too, for Paul. Both married and unmarried persons have the same call to learn what it means truly to love one another. They are different paths to the same goal, each a special gift from God.

In being married, or in our experience of those who are married, we are reminded of the special relationship that exists between Christ and the church. Paul writes about this as a "deep secret truth" that is being revealed – a revelation of how "Christ loved the church and gave himself for it" Eph 5:25 (RSV). The family is a model of God's family, the church. All of us are called to be part of this family, and in our married or single states we bring different gifts to it.

In being single, or in our experience of those who are single, we are reminded of the special relationship that exists between Christ and the individual. Paul saw his single state as enabling him to give himself more completely to God and to his work. Each of us has to make our own decision to open up our life to God and to others; each of us has ultimately to take responsibility for our own attitudes, choices, and actions. We each decide the extent or limits of our own growth into mature personhood. There is an "aloneness", which we often experience as loneliness that no other person, possession, or accomplishment can satisfy. Ultimately only God can satisfy this deep longing within. This is a mystery too – a revelation of the unique relationship between each individual and God.

GOD HAS POURED...HIS LOVE INTO OUR HEARTS/Rom 5:5 (NIV) — **TWENTY-SIXTH**

HOW WIDE AND LONG AND HIGH AND DEEP IS THE LOVE OF CHRIST/Eph 3:18 (NIV) — **TWENTY-SEVENTH**

LOVE EACH OTHER AS I HAVE LOVED YOU/Jn 15:12 (NIV) — **TWENTY-EIGHTH**

SERVE ONE ANOTHER IN LOVE/Gal 5:13 (NIV) — **TWENTY-NINTH**

LOVE BUILDS UP/1 Cor 8:1 (NIV) — **THIRTIETH**

OVERFLOW MORE AND MORE WITH LOVE FOR OTHERS/Phil 1:9 (LB) — **THIRTY-FIRST**

DON'T JUST PRETEND THAT YOU LOVE OTHERS, REALLY LOVE THEM/Rom 12:9 (LB) — **FIRST**

WEEK THIRTY-SIX

SECOND	PRAY FOR USA
THIRD	USA
FOURTH	USA
FIFTH	CANADA
SIXTH	CANADA
SEVENTH	ALASKA
EIGHTH	FOR HUMAN CONTACT, FOR COURAGE AND VISION THAT BRING PEOPLE TOGETHER IN LOVING EMBRACE – WE GIVE THANKS. (United Church, Toronto)

O God, who has bound us together in this bundle of life, give us grace to understand how our lives depend upon the courage, the industry, the honesty and the integrity of our fellow human beings, that we may be mindful of their needs, grateful for their faithfulness, and faithful in our responsibilities to them...

This prayer of Reinhold Niebuhr was first published in 1939. "It is no accident," writes John Carden, compiler of *With All God's People*, "that one of the first modern devotional acknowledgements of our human interdependence should come out of a nation rich in human potential, material resources and political significance."

These same concerns were taken up in the prayers for the North American continent in 1986 at the World Day of Prayer for Peace in Assisi:

We pray for the peoples of the North American continent that they may be renewed in the Christian ideals of justice and freedom, so that they may be ever more aware of their responsibilities in the family of nations and that they may give themselves to the needs of others, with respect for their aspirations and compassion for their needs, and themselves ever be just stewards of what has been entrusted to them.

In Canada this same theme of interdependence finds a particular expression in the concern to discover what it means to be a truly multi-cultural nation – to find a way of living together as French – and English-speaking Canadians, and increasingly to share their home with those of other nationalities who seek a place of their own in this vast land.

The apostle Peter told Jesus he was willing to go to prison with him, and even to die with him. But Jesus knew better; he warned Peter that he didn't really know himself.

It was a very different Peter whom Jesus met on the shore of Galilee after the resurrection. Peter knew himself better now, and Jesus knew he could trust him with his true vocation. "Feed my sheep". Jesus, who saw Peter's weakness, saw also his true giftedness.

Read the story again this week in the passages given each day.

God is very gentle with us. He reveals to us what is helpful for us to know about ourselves, when the time is right for us to grasp it. But sometimes we are afraid to face the truth about ourselves and prefer to hide behind a kind of false piety. Like Peter, we protest. "That is not true about me." And we hide the truth from ourselves (rarely from others!) – until the next time weakness trips us up.

Such self-knowledge is not in order that we may become more centered on ourselves, but – as a snake sheds its skin – to help us shed the false-self and find underneath the true self. It is this true self which is the image of God reflected *through me*.

PETER'S STORY Read Lk 5:1-10   **NINTH**

ReadMk 3:16   **TENTH**

Read Mt 16:13-19   **ELEVENTH**

Read Mt 16:21-23   **TWELFTH**

Read Jn 13:3-9   **THIRTEENTH**

Read Mt 26:31-35, 69-75   **FOURTEENTH**

Read Jn 21:15-22   **FIFTEENTH**

WEEK THIRTY-EIGHT

SIXTEENTH   PRAY FOR THE CHILDREN TO WHOM YOU ARE RELATED

SEVENTEENTH   – CHILDREN OF FRIENDS

EIGHTEENTH   – CHILDREN IN YOUR CHURCH

NINETEENTH   – CHILDREN IN YOUR NEIGHBORHOOD

TWENTIETH   – CHILDREN OF YOUR NATION

TWENTY-FIRST   – CHILDREN OF THE WORLD

TWENTY-SECOND   HUMANITY OWES TO THE CHILD THE BEST IT CAN GIVE
                                    (United Nations Declaration)

"I'm a person too, just like you", a child protested.

As adults we can sometimes make children feel that they don't exist, that we don't like them or are just not interested in what they feel or have to say. All of us have a gift to give to children.

We can give them the gift of just being there. We can make ourselves available by not being too busy, sometimes just sitting down in the same room, being quiet, but present. Often quietly getting on with some activity or game of our own – doing a jigsaw puzzle, drawing a picture, making some sweets – will encourage a shy child to ask if he or she can "do it too".

We can give them the gift of attention. We can listen, not talk. All children have a lot to say, if there is someone to listen. Perhaps you sense a child is bothered about something and needs to talk but can't. Suggest a walk or an outing together. The relaxed atmosphere will make communication easier. If they tell you something you disapprove of, don't over-react. Children need to grow through different phases. Gently drawing them out about how they feel in a matter-of-fact sort of way is the best support to give.

We can give them the gift of affirmation, the sense of their own personhood, their own value. Don't always give advice. Instead ask "What do you think you should do?" Never give a child the message that she or he is bad: "You are a messy", "You are a naughty person", "You don't love me". The same message can be given by saying, "I don't like it when you make a mess", or "I felt hurt by that". Don't give a child the impression that what he says is silly or stupid; instead, tell your young friend what it is you like and enjoy about him, how much you love her and enjoy her company.

God, grant that in my mother tongue
Thy gospel may be sounded,
To rich and poor, to old and young
Its blessings be expounded,
Over vale and glen
By lip and pen,
To each remotest dwelling,
While thy strong hand
Safeguards our land,
Dangers and foes repelling.

Icelandic Christians prepare to commemorate one thousand years of Christianity in the year 2000. Amongst their national treasures are these three-hundred year old passion hymns of Hallgrimur Petersson. They are read aloud in homes throughout Lent, and recited on the radio after the evening news.

Prayer for safety from dangers and foes is common to all these Nordic countries. Here where East and West meet, a concern has grown to promote worldwide justice and international peace. From Sweden comes the prayer:

Destroy, O Lord, the spirit of self-seeking in individuals and nations. Give to the peoples and their leaders thoughts of peace and reconciliation. For you, O Lord, can find a way where human beings know not what to do.

PRAY FOR ICELAND	**TWENTY-THIRD**
DENMARK	**TWENTY-FOURTH**
GREENLAND	**TWENTY-FIFTH**
FINLAND	**TWENTY-SIXTH**
NORWAY	**TWENTY-SEVENTH**
SWEDEN	**TWENTY-EIGHTH**

GOD, OUR CREATOR, HELP US TO BECOME CHANGED PEOPLE, **TWENTY-NINTH**
AND TO CHANGE OUR ATTITUDES.
(Prayer from Finland)

WEEK FORTY

THIRTIETH   WHAT IS IMPORTANT TO YOU?

FIRST   WHAT ARE YOUR VALUES?

SECOND   WHAT ATTIITUDES ARE CHANGING?

THIRD   WHAT SUSTAINS YOU?

FOURTH   WHAT DREAMS ARE UNFULFILLED?

FIFTH   WHO ARE YOU REALLY?

SIXTH   BECOME MATURE, ATTAINING TO THE WHOLE MEASURE OF THE FULNESS OF
CHRIST/Eph 4:13 (NIV)

Autumn is that season that creeps up on us unawares. The signs may cause us to catch our breath and wonder. We had not realized how quickly the year was passing, and our awareness of it may stir deeper feelings – the sense of our own mortality.

Autumn, however, will woo us into acceptance and renewed activity. There is about autumn a richness, a warmth, an abundance that brings comfort and gives strength. The colors of autumn are those that give depth and substance. There are fruits to gather and enjoy, and in gathering them we notice already within them the seeds of new growth.

In the season of our own lives, autumn represents mid-life. Questions begin to surface: What have I accomplished? What are the dreams that have not been realized? What lies still hidden in me, untouched and unrealized as yet? What is life really about? We need to give adequate time to find our own answers to these questions.

An awareness that there are pressing questions to be answered is likely to catch us unawares too. The questions will come when it is the right time for us to attend to them. In answering the questions, time will again begin to stretch like a piece of elastic. Suddenly there is so much more to do and to enjoy. There is indeed new growth hidden within the fruitfulness of our own lives.

What is experienced at mid-life is also experienced by all of us throughout our lives mid-way through any task or life situation. When the questions begin to press, it is time to stop and answer them.

WEEK FORTY-ONE

SEVENTH   MY LORD, I AM YOURS

EIGHTH   YOU ARE...THE SOURCE OF JOY

NINTH   ...GIVE ME PERFECT LOVE

TENTH   GOD, BE MERCIFUL TO ME, A SINNER

ELEVENTH   LORD, SHOW ME POVERTY, WHOM YOU LOVE SO DEARLY

TWELFTH   KEEP NOTHING BACK FOR YOURSELVES

THIRTEENTH   "HE WHO CALLED NOTHING ON EARTH HIS OWN, OWNED
                         EVERYTHING, AND GOD IN EVERYTHING."
                                               (Bonaventure)

All praise be yours, my Lord
in all your creatures,
especially Sir Brother Sun
who brings the day;
and light you give us through him.
How beautiful he is, how radiant in his splendour!
Of you, Most High, he is the token.

Francis of Assisi made it a personal discipline to let his waking thoughts be praise to God, and in particular praise to God for the rising of the sun. He encouraged others to do the same. "*In the morning when the sun rises, everyone ought to praise God who created it for our use, because thanks to it our eyes are enlightened by day...*"

The first part of the famous *Canticle of the Creatures*, from which this verse is taken, was written at a time when Francis was seriously ill and suffering from depression. Later in life when he again suffered from severe illness he sang the Canticle and invited others to join him in its praise to God. Praising God was the strongest antidote to Francis' sadness and depression.

There is a renewed interest in Francis among Christians today. His merriness, his joy, the delight he took in the earth, flowers, plants, and animals, his spontaneity that often expressed itself in singing and dancing – captures our imagination. For Francis, however, this exuberance was the outcome of a life that embraced simplicity, poverty, service to the poor, suffering, pain, and death. In a materialistic age, Francis reminds us that to live life fully is not to depend upon possessions or outward circumstances, but upon an attitude that finds and serves God in all things.

Francis is remembered this month on 4 October, and the day-to-day sayings are from his writings.

"Send your Holy Spirit on us all, we pray, now and ever anew, that the Spirit may awaken us, illumine us, encourage and give us the strength to dare to take the small yet gigantic step, to leave behind the comfort with which we can comfort ourselves and to step forward in to the hope that is in you.

"That nations and their governments may submit to your Word and be willing to strive for justice and peace on earth.

"That, through your word and deed, your Word may be rightly told to all who are poor, all who are sick, all prisoners, all who are in distress, all those who are oppressed, all who do not believe; that they may hear it and understand it and heed it as your answer to their groans and cries.

"That Christians of all churches and confessions may understand your Word with new eyes and learn to serve it with renewed faithfulness."

Karl Barth's Prayer at Pentecost focuses our prayers this week for these three alpine countries. Geographically they have been a strategic link between east and west, and all three have maintained a policy of active neutrality. Here a number of well known international organisations, such as the Red Cross, have been able to make their home.

PRAY FOR AUSTRIA	**FOURTEENTH**
AUSTRIA	**FIFTEENTH**
LIECHTENSTEIN	**SIXTEENTH**
SWITZERLAND	**SEVENTEENTH**
SWITZERLAND	**EIGHTEENTH**
LET OUR CHIEF END, O GOD, BE TO GLORIFY THEE	**NINETEENTH**
AND LET OUR SECOND ENDEAVOUR BE TO SHARE WITH OTHERS WHAT WE SO RICHLY ENJOY. (After Calvin's Catechism)	**TWENTIETH**

WEEK FORTY-THREE

TWENTY-ONE   AGING – IS A BASIS FOR HOPE

TWENTY-TWO   – IS A GRADUAL MATURING

TWENTY-THREE   – IS A CHANCE TO BE EMBRACED

TWENTY-FOUR   – BREAKS THROUGH ARTIFICIAL BOUNDARIES

TWENTY-FIVE   – LEADS US TO DISCOVER MORE AND MORE OF LIFE'S TREASURES

TWENTY-SIX   – IS THE GRADUAL FULFILMENT OF THE LIFE CYCLE

TWENTY-SEVEN   – IS A PROCESS OF GROWTH BY WHICH THE MYSTERY OF LIFE IS SLOWLY REVEALED TO US

People are living longer. In industrialized countries we can now expect to live well into our seventies and possibly well beyond this, whereas thirty years ago life expectancy was the late sixties. Life expectancy is also growing in other parts of the world, as living conditions improve.

How do you feel about growing older? Do you fear it? What kind of person do you hope to be when you are ten, twenty, thirty years older than you are now? What are your conceptions of old age? Where do they come from? Are your images fed by books or the media or people you know? What kind of person would you like to be? Think of an older person you admire. What do you admire about her or him? What do you learn from the example of this person about the possibilities of your own aging?

What do you feel about dying? Most of us draw back from thinking about this. There is, however, a strong Christian tradition that encourages us prayerfully to reflect on our own death. What is it like to say goodbye to those you love? To your own body? To let go of this life in order to embrace what is beyond? Imagine yourself standing with Jesus as a spectator at your own funeral. What are people feeling, saying? What is Jesus saying to you? What do you say to him?

Facing the future in this way can paradoxically free us to live the present moment to the fullest, since we have faced whatever foreboding or fears we had and seen both through and beyond them.

The day-to day sayings this week are taken from *Aging: The Fulfilment of Life* by Henri Nouen and Walter Gaffney.

I have calmed and quieted my soul.
Ps. 131:2 (RSV)

Do you weave into your prayers and into your days times when you are just still and quiet? Have you learned how healing and yet energising contemplative prayer – the prayer of simple quiet – is?

One Christian has described this kind of prayer as "Just sitting with Jesus". How we sit to do this is important. Sit upright in a chair that supports your back; don't slump. Listen to all the sounds you can hear. Now concentrate on your breathing. Breathe slowly, deeply, and regularly. Become aware of the different parts of your body, particularly those parts that are tense. Stretch and relax those parts. A stillness and a quietness will come.

In this time of quiet contemplation, few or any words are needed. This is companionship that is felt in silence. Meditation on a word or sentence from the Scriptures or from a prayer or hymn may be an aid to this. Or, in the silence, a word or sentence may come to you. If so, meditate quietly on that.

Weaving times of silence into your day or week is helpful too. Decide that there are times when you turn the radio or TV off. Accustom yourself to silence. Families can build silence into their lives too. A hour or thirty minutes a day when the radio and TV is turned off, when conversation is limited to only what is absolutely necessary. Make this time a special time for children – a time when they learn to enjoy books or to play quietly.

There is a deep companionship that grows in silence – not only between us and God, but within a family and between friends too.

The day-to-day sayings this week are taken from *Contemplating Jesus* by Robert Faricy, S.J. and Robert Wicks.

CONTEMPLATION – IS PAYING ATTENTION TO THE LORD — **TWENTY-EIGHTH**

– INVOLVES RELATIONSHIP — **TWENTY-NINTH**

– IS A WAY OF LOOKING AT JESUS WITH LOVE — **THIRTIETH**

– IS OPENING MY HEART TO HIS LOVE — **THIRTY-FIRST**

– IS KNOWLEDGE OF JESUS THROUGH LOVE — **FIRST**

– IS A GIFT FROM GOD — **SECOND**

WHAT IS IMPORTANT IN CONTEMPLATION IS THE *HEART,* NOT SO MUCH THE HEAD — **THIRD**

WEEK FORTY-FIVE

FOURTH   PRAY FOR POLAND

FIFTH   CZECHOSLOVAKIA

SIXTH   HUNGARY, ROMANIA

SEVENTH   YUGOSLAVIA

EIGHTH   ALBANIA, BULGARIA

NINTH   MONGOLIA, U S S R

TENTH   O LORD, IN YOU HAVE I TRUSTED: LET ME NEVER BE CONFOUNDED.

(5th Century, Yugoslavia)

Khristos voskress! Christ is risen!
Voistinu voskrese He is risen indeed
Christ is risen from the dead: trampling down death by death;
and upon those in the tombs bestowing life. Though you
descended into the grave, O Immortal One, yet you put down
the power of Hades, and rose as conqueror, O Christ our God:
you spoke clearly to the myrrh-bearing women, Rejoice: you
bestowed peace upon your apostles, and to the fallen you
brought resurrection. Russian Orthodox

The 1990s began with scenes of huge demonstrations on the streets of many East European countries. One country after the other returned to religious freedom and democratic rule. In all these countries the church played a crucial role, supporting the people's movements for freedom and contributing to the largely non-violent overthrow of totalitarian rule.

Those countries with national and personal freedoms restored face immense problems of how to build new social structures that combine freedom for the individual and a just sharing of common resources. In this they seek to find new and creative methods forward that will help us all. From Yugoslavia comes the prayer:

Lord, you sent your Son Jesus Christ into the
world to reconcile us to yourself and to one another.
Help us to know how to work together with Christ
towards the achievement of universal reconciliation.

And be thankful. Col. 3:15 (NIV)

Learning how to live in a spirit of thankfulness for all that we receive from God day by day can make all the difference between really living or merely existing.

Saying "Thank you" however can be a part of our praying that has little or no real content. From time to time, therefore, it is helpful to focus on thanksgiving. One way of doing this is to write down in your journal at the end of each day three things for which you are particularly grateful. If you do this for a month, you will be delighted at how many things come to mind. Repeat this from time to time, particularly at those times when you sense life for you has become rather grey.

Another way is to take a day of the week when you resolve to take the day slowly, giving time to each chore or task, being appreciative of what you handle and see. A day when you take time just to be with people, to appreciate friends and neighbors. A day of mindfulness, of thankfulness.

November is the month in America when a day of Thanksgiving is observed. Many American families observe this day in their own homes, and make the traditional thanksgiving meal a time for each person present to talk about those things they are most thankful for as they look back over the year. Pictures, postcards, photographs, mementos all can be used by children and adults to make this sharing time particularly memorable and enjoyable. It is a tradition we can all observe.

Focusing on saying thanks helps us to remember how much God has given us to enrich life, and to become better stewards of his creation.

GIVE THANKS TO HIM AND PRAISE HIS NAME/Ps 100:4 (NIV) — **ELEVENTH**

IT IS GOOD TO SAY "THANK YOU" TO THE LORD/Ps 92:1 (LB) — **TWELFTH**

ALWAYS BE FULL OF JOY IN THE LORD/Phil 4:4 (LB) — **THIRTEENTH**

ALWAYS GIVE THANKS FOR EVERYTHING/Eph 5:20 (NIV) — **FOURTEENTH**

GIVE THANKS IN ALL CIRCUMSTANCES/1 Thess 5:18 (NIV) — **FIFTEENTH**

MY THANKS WILL BE HIS PRAISE/Ps 69:30 (LB) — **SIXTEENTH**

EVERYTHING GOD CREATED IS GOOD...AND TO BE RECEIVED WITH THANKSGIVING/1 Tim 4:4 (NIV) — **SEVENTEENTH**

"You're just like your mother." "Grandfather always used to do that too."

All families have family traits, attitudes, ways of speaking, doing things, dealing with or avoiding problems. Some of these family traits surface at the most inappropriate moments; traits or attitudes we may unconsciously have never recognised in ourselves or that we think we had repudiated.

Family traits and habits are always a mixture of good and bad, helpful and unhelpful, strengths and weaknesses. Usually we are prepared to own the strengths, but prefer the weaknesses to be kept hidden. These are those skeletons in the cupboard that are not talked about. Once in a while it is good to open the cupboard door, and let some light in. Then strengths can be seen for what they are and welcomed, weaknesses for what they are and their power broken.

Taking a look at one's "family script" can be done in a gentle and even playful way. What are the family strengths? Each family member make their own list, and then each in turn reads it out. See how much you agree? Then, make a list of family weaknesses. Again, read out the lists and see where you agree or disagree. Are there some weaknesses that you don't want to continue to compound?

The conversation is underway. Just talking about such family traits or scripts is a growing point for any family. If it is inappropriate to do it as a family group, two or more members căn do it together, or you can do the exercise just for your own benefit.

YOU SAW ME BEFORE I WAS BORN	**EIGHTEENTH**
YOU...KNOW EVERYTHING ABOUT ME	**NINETEENTH**
YOU ARE THINKING ABOUT ME CONSTANTLY	**TWENTIETH**
YOU KNOW WHEN I SIT OR STAND	**TWENTY-FIRST**
YOU CHART THE PATH AHEAD OF ME	**TWENTY-SECOND**
YOU...PLACE YOUR HAND OF BLESSING ON MY HEAD	**TWENTY-THIRD**
YOUR WORKMANSHIP IS MARVELLOUS...THANK YOU FOR MAKING ME SO WONDERFULLY COMPLEX. Ps 139 (LB)	**TWENTY-FOURTH**

WEEK FORTY-EIGHT

TWENTY-FIFTH   TO MAKE READY A PEOPLE PREPARED FOR THE LORD/Lk 1:17 (NIV)

TWENTY-SIXTH   IN THE PAST GOD SPOKE...THROUGH THE PROPHETS/Heb 1:1 (NIV)

TWENTY-SEVENTH   (John the Baptist shouted): PREPARE A ROAD FOR THE LORD TO
TRAVEL ON/Lk 3:6 (LB)

TWENTY-EIGHTH   (Mary said) GOD...HAS LIFTED UP THE HUMBLE/Lk 1:52 (NIV)

TWENTY-NINTH   HE (Jesus) WILL NOT JUDGE BY APPEARANCE/Is 11:3 (LB)

THIRTIETH   HE WILL DEFEND THE POOR AND EXPLOITED/Is 11:4 (LB)

FIRST   SO SHALL THE EARTH BE FULL OF THE KNOWLEDGE OF THE
LORD/Is 11:9 (LB)

As Christmas approaches we become more and more aware of all the secular preparations for this day. In the midst of all of this, how do we keep in mind the deeper meaning of Christ's birthday?

One way is to observe the season of Advent as a time for personal and family reflection. An advent wreath can help us to do this. This is a simple wreath made of holly or evergreen entwined around a circular band of metal, wood, or wire, and containing five candles – one in the center, the others in a circle around this center candle.

The season of Advent covers the four Sundays preceding Christmas. One candle is lit the first Sunday, two the second, three the third, four the fourth, and the center one on Christmas Day.

A number of different themes are associated with the four Sundays in Advent. One is to reflect the first Sunday on the theme of hope, the second on peace, the third on joy, and the fourth on love. Another is to take the four themes of: God's people awaiting Jesus' coming, the prophets who foretold it, John the Baptist who prepared the way, and Mary, who gave him birth.

To make this your own personal of family time of reflection and preparation, choose your own Scripture readings for each Sunday, following one of these themes. Each Sunday also reflect on your own response to those readings. For example, what gives you hope? What do you hope for in the coming year? Or what is your experience of being part of the people of God? Who are those who have prepared the way for his coming in your life?

Christmas Day, when the final candle is lit, the theme is Christ the light of the world. What does it mean for Jesus to be born in you? How is that life growing in you? In what ways do you share his light with others?

Those countries joining together to form a greater economic and political cohesion within Europe do so in the hope that long-term peaceful cooperation will replace its long history of conflict and war. There is, however, the fear that this emphasis on market forces will be to the detriment of the many poor and marginalized people within Europe itself, and globally that Europe could become a "fortress", looking only to its own interests and not taking its full part in contributing to a new world order where the concerns of one are the concerns of all.

This is a particular concern of many Christians within Europe, who pray:

Our God, we are one in solidarity with those who live in danger and struggle.

Whether near or far, we share their anguish and their hope.

Teach us to extend our lives beyond ourselves and to reach out in sympathy to the frontiers where people are suffering and changing the world.

Make us one in solidarity with the aliens we ignore, the deprived we pretend do not exist, the prisoners we avoid.

God, let solidarity be a new contemporary word for this community into which you are constantly summoning us.

We ask it in the name of him who was resolutely in solidarity with abandoned, despised humankind, Jesus Christ your son, our brother.

100 Prières Possibles, André Dumas

DECEMBER

PRAY FOR FRANCE — **SECOND**

REPUBLIC OF IRELAND — **THIRD**

BELGIUM, LUXEMBOURG, HOLLAND — **FOURTH**

GERMANY — **FIFTH**

ITALY, MALTA — **SIXTH**

PORTUGAL, SPAIN — **SEVENTH**

GO NOW ALL OF YOU, IN PEACE TO THE PLACE — **EIGHTH**
WHERE GOD HAS GIVEN YOU RESPONIBILITY AND HE HIMSELF WILL
BLESS YOU, THE FATHER, THE SON, AND THE HOLY SPIRIT
(Huub Oosterhuis)

WEEK FIFTY

NINTH YOU HELP US BY MEANS OF YOUR PRAYERS/2 Cor 1:11 (GNB)

TENTH PRAY ALWAYS FOR ALL GOD'S PEOPLE/Eph 6:18 (GNB)

ELEVENTH I URGE THAT...PRAYERS BE OFFERED TO GOD FOR ALL PEOPLE/1 Tim 2:2 (GNB)

TWELFTH –FOR ALL THAT ARE IN AUTHORITY/1 Tim 2:2 (GNB)

THIRTEENTH PRAY CONTINUALLY/1 Thess 5:17 (NIV)

FOURTEENTH THE HOLY SPIRIT HELPS US...IN OUR PRAYING.../Rom 8:25 (LB)

FIFTEENTH ...WITH SUCH FEELING IT CANNOT BE EXPRESSED IN WORDS/Rom 8:26 (LB)

You are always in my heart Phil. 1:7 (GNB)

Paul the apostle wrote this to the Philippian Christians. His letters show him to be a person of deep prayer for others; an intercessor.

True intercessory prayer is an attitude of the heart, an attitude that we can all nurture. There are simple everyday things that we can do to help us become intercessors.

Simple things like an arrangement of photographs, a collection of postcards, a child's drawing – building around us in our homes a visual reminder of our network of family and friends. As we dust and sweep, we can pray. Or just sit and look, remember and pray.

We can do simple things like standing in a bus line or sitting in a car in a traffic jam, and using that as an opportunity for prayer. Start off by praying for the people passing by. Ask God to lead your thoughts and your prayers. You will find yourself identifying with these people, this place – the kind of identification that can challenge, raise questions, disturb. This too is part of intercession.

A world map on the wall can remind us to pray. Stop by it from time to time and take a trip around the world. What do you know of these countries, these people? Listen to the world news, read the newspaper with the desire to learn more, to understand better, to see what God sees and to feel as he feels for the peoples and the nations of the world.

To intercede in this way is also to say to God, "Is there some response you want from me, some task for me to do?".

DECEMBER

SIXTEENTH THERE IS A TIME FOR EVERYTHING– A TIME TO PLANT AND A TIME TO UPROOT

SEVENTEENTH – A TIME TO TEAR DOWN AND A TIME TO HEAL

EIGHTEENTH – A TIME TO WEEP AND A TIME TO LAUGH

NINETEENTH – A TIME TO SCATTER STONES AND A TIME TO GATHER THEM UP

TWENTIETH – A TIME TO SEARCH AND A TIME TO GIVE UP

TWENTY-FIRST – A TIME TO KEEP AND A TIME TO THROW AWAY/Eccl 3:2-8 (NIV)

TWENTY-SECOND TEACH US TO NUMBER OUR DAYS THAT WE MAY GET A HEART OF WISDOM/Ps 90:12 (RSV)

"Love winter when the plant says nothing."

As the night closes in on us and the days become shorter, we may be bracing ourselves to live through another winter. It will bring its own delights: times of seasonal celebration; time for playing indoor games, watching television, for reading, home hobbies, crafts and do-it-yourself projects.

It is a time of hiddenness and of endings. Within our own life seasons and throughout our lives – as we experience the different endings of school, college, of a job or a change of location, as friends move away or we experience bereavement, as children grow older and leave home – so in all these lesser deaths we learn or maybe fail to learn how to live with closure. In learning how to let go, we discover that underneath there is a greater gift awaiting us. In this way even into old age we discover how inexhaustible are the gifts that God has in store for us.

As each winter comes it is a helpful thing to ask ourselves the question: What is dying in my life this year? What must I let go of?

*Let us not be disheartened,
even when the horizon of history grows dim and
closes in, as though human realities made
impossible the accomplishment of God's plans.
God makes use even of our errors, even of our sins,
so as to make rise over the darkness what Isaiah
spoke of.
One day prophets will sing not only the return
from Babylon but our full liberation.
"The people that walked in darkness have seen a
great light."
They walk in lands of shadows, but a light has
shone forth. (Is 9:1-12)*

These words were written by Oscar Romero,
who was for three years the Archbishop of San Salvador
until his martyrdom in his own cathedral in 1980. He
was killed for his brave defense of the poor and of those
oppressed and tortured in their own land. He wrote the
above on Christmas Day 1977. The message of
Christmas gave him hope for the future.

What special meaning has Christ's birth for
you this Christmas? See if you, too, can capture in prose
or verse your response to a Scripture verse, a hymn, or a
thought that you have had about his coming.

YOU (MARY) ARE THE MOST BLESSED OF ALL WOMEN/Lk 1:42 (GNB)   **TWENTY-THIRD**

AND BLESSED IS THE CHILD YOU WILL BEAR/Lk 1:42 (GNB)   **TWENTY-FOURTH**

THIS DAY...YOUR SAVIOR WAS BORN, CHRIST THE LORD/Lk 2:11 (GNB)   **TWENTY-FIFTH**

GLORY TO GOD IN THE HIGHEST HEAVEN/Lk 2:14 (GNB)   **TWENTY-SIXTH**

AND PEACE ON EARTH TO THOSE WITH WHOM HE IS PLEASED/Lk 2:14 (GNB)   **TWENTY-SEVENTH**

LORD, YOU HAVE KEPT YOUR PROMISE/Lk 2:29 (GNB)   **TWENTY-EIGHTH**

I HAVE SEEN YOUR SALVATION, WHICH YOU HAVE PREPARED IN THE PRESENCE OF ALL PEOPLES/Lk 2:30, 31 (GNB)   **TWENTY-NINTH**

WEEK FIFTY-THREE

THIRTIETH   YOUR FAITHFULNESS CONTINUES THROUGH ALL GENERATIONS/Ps 119:90
(NIV)

THIRTY-FIRST   THE STEADFAST LOVE OF THE LORD NEVER CEASES/Lam 3:22 (RSV)

A review of the past is the best way to prepare for the future.

What kind of year has this been for you? What have been the significant happenings? What have you most enjoyed? What have been your disappointments? In what ways have you grown and matured as a person?

From time to time it is also helpful to look back further into the past, to recall and share one's life story with others. As families it is important to do this, and also as communities and congregations.

Telling our story can be the theme one Sunday for a church congregation, weaving in stories from the past with hymns and readings that tell of God's faithfulness. Families and smaller groups can find more intimate ways to share stories. Each person can bring a photograph, a letter, or some other personal memento and share the story behind that. Younger members learn more about their own family or group story. Close by asking the question: What have we remembered that is helpful to us as we look to the future?

The desire to recall and share the past comes naturally as we grow older. While a preoccupation with the past is unhelpful, this need to reflect on and share the past is an important way in which we gain wisdom and pass it on to the next generation. A family, group, or congregation can collect stories from senior members, interviewing and recording the stories as a valued resource for the future. In their teens young people often begin to ask questions about the past; the task of interviewing is one many of them will welcome and enjoy.

The value we give to the past is the value we also give to the future.